Read & Respond

FOR
KS1

Read & Respond

FOR
KS1

Author: Louise Carruthers

Development Editor: Simret Brar

Editor: Vicky Butt

Assistant Editor: Margaret Eaton

Series Designer: Anna Oliwa

Designer: Shelley Best

Cover image: Marcus Pfister

Illustrations: Marcus Pfister, Baz Rowell

Text © 2008 Louise Carruthers © 2008 Scholastic Ltd

Designed using Adobe InDesign

Published by Scholastic Ltd, Villiers House,
Clarendon Avenue, Leamington Spa,
Warwickshire CV32 5PR

www.scholastic.co.uk

Printed by Bell & Bain

1 2 3 4 5 6 7 8 9   8 9 0 1 2 3 4 5 6 7

British Library Cataloguing-in-Publication Data
A catalogue record for this book is available from the British Library.

ISBN 978-1407-10039-5

Acknowledgements
NordSüd Verlag AG for the use of extracts and illustrations from *The Rainbow Fish* by Marcus Pfister © 1992, Marcus Pfister (1992, NordSüd).

The Rainbow Fish

About the book

The Rainbow Fish is a superbly illustrated book renowned for the stunning watercolour illustrations and shimmering holographs that bring the story to life.

The central character is a beautiful but conceited fish who has sparkling blue, green, purple and silver shimmering scales. When the other fish ask him to share his shiny scales, he refuses. This causes the other fish to shun his company as they swim about in the ocean together.

Feeling lonely and upset, the Rainbow Fish turns to a wise octopus for advice. She tells him to share his glittering scales with the other fish. The Rainbow Fish is unsure but decides to follows the octopus's advice. He is surprised and delighted to discover that the octopus was right. The more he shares, the happier he becomes as the other fish finally accept him as their friend.

Perfect for teaching children about friendship and sharing, this versatile text is also an ideal stimulus for a wide range of activities linked to the PNS key objectives (Foundation–Year 2).

Active exploration of the fantasy underwater setting, engaging characters and the simple plot structure make ideal starting points for a range of fiction and non-fiction writing activities, including character profiles, instructional texts and setting descriptions.

Children's speaking and listening ability can be developed through a variety of drama, role play and discussion activities linked to the text.

The Rainbow Fish can also be used to teach a variety of word and sentence level objectives. The text contains many of the Key Stage 1 high frequency words. It includes examples of compound words and words containing a range of the long vowel phonemes taught at KS1.

About the author

Marcus Pfister was born in Berne, Switzerland, where he trained as a graphic artist and designer. His first book, *The Sleepy Owl*, was published in 1986.

Before becoming an author and illustrator, Marcus Pfister worked as a graphic designer in an advertising agency in Zurich. He has written and illustrated a number of well-known books for children, including the *Penguin Pete* and *Hopper the Rabbit* series of books. Many of his books tackle important moral issues such as sharing, consideration, friendship and taking responsibility.

The Rainbow Fish is probably the book for which Marcus Pfister is best known. The Rainbow Fish also features in four other titles by Pfister, including *Rainbow Fish to the Rescue* (1995) and *The Rainbow Fish Finds his Way* (2006).

Marcus Pfister writes his stories in German. They are then translated into other languages and sold around the world. His picture books are generally illustrated with pen drawings and pastel watercolours. A distinctive feature of many of his books is holographic foil stamping, which is used to create pictures that have a reflective effect when held in the light.

> **Facts and figures**
> *The Rainbow Fish* has been published in more than 30 languages around the world. It is a winner of several children's book awards.

Guided reading

2

Cover illustration and text

Introduce the shared text. Marvel at the beautiful fish illustrated on the front cover and pass the book around the group to give each child an opportunity to look closely at and feel the special holographic scales.

Encourage the children to make simple predictions about the story. Where do they think the story is going to take place? Do they think the fish will be the main character in the story? How do they think the fish is feeling? Where is he going? What other characters do they think might be in the story?

Ask the children to identify and read the title of the story. Consider why 'Rainbow Fish' is an appropriate name for the fish pictured on the front cover.

Talk about the other information that is given on the front cover. Use the terms 'author' and 'publisher'. Ask the children to recall whether they have read any other stories written by Marcus Pfister.

The blurb

Remind children of the term 'blurb' and its purpose. Talk about where in a book the blurb can be found. Turn to the back cover and read the blurb together. Ask the children to consider whether the information given makes them want to read the book. Talk about the role of the publisher in promoting and selling the book, and the need to make it sound appealing. What information has been included in the blurb to make the reader believe this is a good book? (Positive book reviews and information about awards the book has received.)

Encourage the children to use the information given on the back cover to make other predictions about the story. Who do they think the Rainbow Fish shares his scales with?

Title page

Look at the title page. Ask the children to locate the title, the author's name and the publisher's name. Consider the other information recorded on the title page ('translated by J. Alison James'). Explain to the children that Marcus Pfister writes his stories in German. The stories are then translated into other languages so that people all over the world can enjoy his books.

First reading

In the first reading and exploration of the text it is vital that the children's enjoyment is paramount. Read the story at a fluent reading pace. While reading the story, encourage the children to look closely at the beautiful watercolour illustrations. Ask them to name the underwater creatures and plants that are depicted throughout the story. Stop at relevant points in the story to invite the children to predict what might happen next. Ask questions such as: *Do you think the Rainbow Fish will give the little blue fish one of his scales? What do you think the octopus will tell the Rainbow Fish to do?*

After reading the text for the first time, spend some time talking about the characters. Encourage the children to speculate on their feelings and motives. Ask: *Why was the Rainbow Fish lonely? Why do you think the other fish would not have anything to do with the Rainbow Fish?*

Encourage the children to empathise with the Rainbow Fish by drawing on their own experiences of feeling lonely and upset.

Ascertain the children's first impressions of the book. Did they enjoy the story? Which character did they like best? Why? What do they think of the illustrations?

Subsequent readings

In each subsequent reading of the text, it is important to reinforce and practise key reading skills. In every guided reading session, make sure that you:
● model how to read the text with fluency and expression;
● emphasise directionality and one-to-one correspondence between spoken and written words by following the text with a pointer;

4

READ & RESPOND: Activities based on The Rainbow Fish

● help the children to use a range of decoding strategies (for example, phonological or grammatical knowledge) to read unfamiliar words;
● encourage the children to predict/recall what happens next at different points in the story;
● ask targeted questions to develop the children's understanding of the text.

Story opening

Read the first page together, modelling expression and intonation. Talk about the information contained in this opening section. Consider how Marcus Pfister has used description to introduce the main character and the story setting. Discuss whether the children think this is an effective story opening. Does it make them want to read on? Why?

Turn to the next page. Talk about why the fish with the shiny scales is called the 'Rainbow Fish' by the other fish. Ask the children to suggest other suitable names for him.

Feeling lonely

Continue reading the text with the children to the point where the fish swim away from the Rainbow Fish and refuse to have anything more to do with him. Read the direct speech aloud with appropriate expression. Look at the speech marks and remind the children of their purpose.

Consider the Rainbow Fish's attitude towards the other fish. Why do the children think the Rainbow Fish ignored the other fish? Can they think of some words to describe his behaviour? (Rude, show off, selfish and so on.)

Reflect on the feelings, motives and behaviour of the other fish. Why did they turn away from the Rainbow Fish? Encourage the children to speculate on what they would do if they found themselves in a similar situation.

Good advice

Turn to the next page, starting: 'What good were the dazzling, shimmering scales with no one to

admire them?' Look at the illustration. Ask: *Who is the Rainbow Fish talking to? Can you remember what the Rainbow Fish asked the starfish?* Discuss how the Rainbow Fish is feeling. Encourage the children to talk about their own experiences of feeling lonely to help them develop empathy for the Rainbow Fish.

Once the children have looked at and discussed the illustration, read the text together. Highlight the word 'that'. Discuss why Marcus Pfister has written 'that' in italics. Why does he want to give particular emphasis to this word?

Continue to read from 'The Rainbow Fish found the cave' to 'How could I ever be happy without them?'. Model how to read with expression and intonation appropriate to the punctuation on each page. Emphasise a raised voice at the end of each question and a short pause after the ellipsis.

Encourage the children to imagine how the Rainbow Fish felt when the octopus appeared out of the darkness. (Scared, nervous, surprised and so on.)

Ask the children to describe in their own words exactly what the octopus has told the Rainbow Fish to do. Do they think this is a good idea? Is it possible for the Rainbow Fish to be happy without his shining scales? Ask: *If the Rainbow Fish came to you for advice, what would you tell him to do?*

A change of heart

Turn to the page that begins 'Suddenly he felt…'. Ask: *Are you surprised that the little blue fish has come back? What do you think he might be saying to the Rainbow Fish?*

Read the text together. Ask the children to find evidence in the text that shows that the Rainbow Fish is thinking about giving the little blue fish one of his shiny scales. (For example: 'Wavered', '…maybe I wouldn't miss just one'.) Can the children predict what the Rainbow Fish will do? Turn over the page. Ask questions such as: *Why are the fish smiling? How does the little blue fish feel now?* (For example: excited, grateful, pleased.)

Guided reading

Happy ending

Read from 'The little blue fish whizzed through the ocean with his scale flashing' to the end of the story. Talk about the meaning of unusual vocabulary and phrases. Ask the children to infer what the author means by 'shared his scales left and right', 'felt at home', 'prized possessions', 'happy as a splash'.

Ask: *Do you think the Rainbow Fish was surprised to find that the more scales he gave away, the happier he became? What do you think was making him feel happy?*

Moral of the story

Give the children an opportunity to reflect on the story. Did they enjoy it? Which part did they like best? Did it have a happy ending? Why?

Discuss the children's feelings about the actions and behaviour of the characters in the story. Consider the moral significance of the story and talk about the important underlying themes of friendship and sharing. Encourage the children to share their own personal experiences of friendship and loneliness. Ask questions such as: *How would you feel if nobody wanted to play with you? What would you do if you saw someone being left out on the playground?*

Discuss the children's feelings about the actions and behaviour of the main characters in the story. Ask: *Why do you think the Rainbow Fish didn't want to share his scales? Have you ever wanted to keep something all to yourself?* (For example, favourite sweets or a special toy.) *Do you think the other fish were right to ignore the Rainbow Fish when he would not share his scales? What would you do if one of your friends refused to share their toys with you?*

Retelling and reflection

When you have finished reading the book with the class, invite the children to name and describe the main characters in the story. Discuss where the story takes place, what happens in the story, and why. Pose simple prompting questions to encourage the children to recall the main incidents in the story in the correct order.

Encourage the children to express some simple opinions about the story and illustrations. Ask questions such as: *Did you enjoy the story? Which part did you like best? Did it have a happy ending? Why?*

Talk about who the children think would be the target audience for the book. (For example, parents choosing a bedtime story to read to their child.)

Ask the children to consider why The Rainbow Fish is a good title for the story. Can they suggest any other suitable titles? (For example, 'The Selfish Fish' or 'The Lonely Fish'.)

Shared reading

Extract 1

- Read an enlarged copy of Extract 1, modelling appropriate expression and intonation.
- Ask the children to describe how each character is feeling. Draw attention to significant words and phrases in the text. ('Shocked', 'Get away', 'upset'.)
- Re-read the first five lines of the extract. Highlight the speech marks and talk about their purpose. Underline the direct speech. Note the features of the text that indicate how the dialogue should be read – question marks, exclamation marks and vocabulary ('cried').
- Ask the children to suggest other devices the author could have used to give emphasis to particular parts of the dialogue. (Italics, capitalisation.) Re-write the first five lines of text, using italics and capitalisation to give further indication of how the text should be read.
- Re-read the modified extract several times with groups or individuals playing the part of the Rainbow Fish.
- Highlight the words 'scales', 'Rainbow' and 'away' on the text. Draw attention to the different ways of spelling the 'ai' sound. Generate lists of other words that contain the long vowel phoneme ai/ay/a–e.

Extract 2

- Conceal several key words on Extract 2 with sticky notes (for example, 'scales', 'loneliest', 'troubles', 'like', 'wise'). Read the extract together. Challenge the children to predict the concealed words. Model the use of a range of strategies, such as predicting words from preceding words in sentences, using awareness of the grammar of a sentence, or by using context cues.
- Ask the children to locate and underline the two words in the text that describe the Rainbow Fish's scales. ('dazzling', 'shimmering'.) Identify what these words have in common. (They both end in '-ing'.)
- Brainstorm alternative words ending in '-ing' that could be used to describe the Rainbow Fish's scales. (*Glittering, sparkling, glistening* and so on.) List the children's suggestions on the board.
- Discuss how compound words can be split into two smaller words to help with reading and understanding. Ask the children to locate the compound words in the text extract. ('starfish', 'anybody', 'maybe'.) Help the children to underline the component parts of each word in a different colour.

Extract 3

- Read the extract together, stopping at some words to discuss the strategies used to read them, (for example, phonological knowledge, grammar or context cues).
- While reading, model how to break longer words into syllables for decoding. ('glittering', 'delighted'.)
- Underline the words in the extract which contain the digraph 'wh'. ('whizzed', 'when'.) Generate a list of some other 'wh' words on the whiteboard.
- Underline the sentence 'The Rainbow Fish shared his scales left and right' on the text extract. Ask the children a range of questions, such as: *What does this sentence mean? Why is the Rainbow Fish giving his scales away to the other fish? Can you find a word or phrase in the text that describes how the Rainbow Fish is feeling?* ('delighted', 'felt at home'.) *What do you think is making him feel this way?*
- Highlight all of the adjectives in the extract. Substitute each adjective with an alternative word suggested by the group. Re-read the text extract to check that the words are a suitable fit.

Extract 1

"You want me to give you one of my special scales? Who do you think you are?" cried the Rainbow Fish. "Get away from me!"

Shocked, the little blue fish swam away. He was so upset, he told all his friends what had happened. From then on, no one would have anything to do with the Rainbow Fish. They turned away when he swam by.

Extract 2

What good were the dazzling, shimmering scales with no one to admire them? Now he was the loneliest fish in the entire ocean.

One day he poured out his troubles to the starfish. "I really am beautiful. Why doesn't anybody like me?"

"I can't answer *that* for you," said the starfish. "But if you go beyond the coral reef to a deep cave you will find the wise octopus. Maybe she can help you."

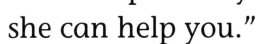

Illustration © 1992, Marcus Pfister

PAGE
9

PHOTOCOPIABLE

READ & RESPOND: Activities based on The Rainbow Fish

Extract 3

The little blue fish whizzed through the ocean with his scale flashing, so it didn't take long before the Rainbow Fish was surrounded by the other fish. Everyone wanted a glittering scale.

The Rainbow Fish shared his scales left and right. And the more he gave away, the more delighted he became. When the water around him filled with glimmering scales, he at last felt at home among the other fish.

Illustration © 1992, Marcus Pfister

Plot, character and setting

The Rainbow Fish

> **Objective:** To give some reasons why things happen or characters change.
> **What you need:** Enlarged set of the word cards on photocopiable page 15, paper and pencils.
> **Cross-curricular links:** PSHE/Citizenship

What to do
● Together with the class, read *The Rainbow Fish*. Pause at significant points in the story to discuss the appearance, qualities and behaviour of the Rainbow Fish.
● Tell the children that you have prepared a set of words to describe the Rainbow Fish at the beginning of the story and a set of words to describe the Rainbow Fish at the end of the story. Explain that the two sets of words have become mixed up and you would like the children to help you sort them out.

● Write the headings 'Beginning' and 'End' on the board. Hold up a word card. Ask the children in pairs to decide whether they think that this word describes the Rainbow Fish at the beginning or end of the story, and why. Pick several pairs to share their ideas. Encourage them to justify their response by referring to events in the story. Repeat until all the words have been sorted.
● Ask the children to write a short description of the Rainbow Fish using some of the adjectives on the board.

> **Differentiation**
> **For older/more confident children:** Ask the children to write about how the feelings and behaviour of the main character change throughout the story.
> **For younger/less confident children:** Draw a picture of the Rainbow Fish. Write some of the descriptive words around the picture.

Problem-resolution stories

> **Objective:** To use key features of narrative in their own writing.
> **What you need:** *The Rainbow Fish*, pencils, a copy of photocopiable page 16 for each child and one enlarged copy.
> **Cross-curricular links:** PSHE

What to do
● Read the story with the children. Track the main plot sequence together:
1) The Rainbow Fish would not share his scales.
2) None of the other fish would have anything to do with the Rainbow Fish. He was lonely.
3) The Rainbow Fish went to ask the octopus for advice.
4) The Rainbow Fish shared his scales with the other fish. He was happy.
● Tell the children that you would like them to plan and write a different story using the same plot structure.

● Ask the children to share times when they had a problem. Who did they turn to for help? What happened? Select an experience recounted by one of the children. Use shared writing to model how to turn the idea into a story plan using the headings on photocopiable page 16. (For example: 'Jake was unhappy at school. None of the children in his class wanted to sit next to him because he distracted them when they were working. Jake asked his teacher for help…'.)
● Let the children plan their own story on a copy of photocopiable page 16.
● In a subsequent lesson, ask them to compose a story using the ideas on their planning sheet.

> **Differentiation**
> **For older/more confident children:** Encourage the children to include narrative and description in their stories.
> **For younger/less confident children:** Let the children tell their stories orally.

Plot, character and setting

Order, order!

> **Objective:** To retell stories, ordering events using story language.
> **What you need:** *The Rainbow Fish*, a copy of the plot cards on photocopiable page 17 for each group and one enlarged copy.
> **Cross-curricular links:** Mathematics

What to do

● Re-read the text together. Encourage the children to recall what happens next at different points in the story and to consider how the main events in the story are connected.

● Work together to sequence a set of plot cards from photocopiable page 17 in the order that the events occur in the story. Refer back to the shared text if necessary.

● Retell the story using the plot cards as prompts. Encourage the children to speak in sentences and to use appropriate time connectives to link the sequence of events.

● Pose a range of questions to develop the children's understanding of time and sequential relationships in the story. For example: *Which card(s) represent what happened at the beginning/ middle/end of the story? Does it matter if I change the order of the cards? Why?*

● Working in small groups, ask the children to order a set of plot cards and then prepare their own retelling of the story. Encourage them to incorporate appropriate time connectives, description and dialogue into their retelling.

> **Differentiation**
> **For older/more confident children:** Ask the children to rewrite the story in order.
> **For younger/less confident children:** Give the children fewer cards to sequence.

In the hot seat

> **Objective:** To explore familiar themes and characters through improvisation and role play.
> **What you need:** *The Rainbow Fish*.
> **Cross-curricular links:** Drama

What to do

● Re-read *The Rainbow Fish* to the point in the story where all of the other fish swim away from the Rainbow Fish because he will not share his special scales. Ask the children to describe the appearance, behaviour and qualities of the Rainbow Fish using words and phrases from the text and expressing their own view. (For example, *proud, beautiful, selfish.*)

● Choose a child to sit in the hot seat and adopt the role of the Rainbow Fish. As a model, take on the role of the little blue fish. Tell the Rainbow Fish how shocked and upset you are that he will not let you have one of his special scales. Ask the rest of the children to pretend to be the other fish. Tell them to let the Rainbow Fish know how they are feeling, and why.

● Encourage the children to ask the Rainbow Fish some appropriate questions to try to find out why he does not want to share his special scales with them.

● Let the Rainbow Fish respond to the comments and questions. For example: *I don't care what you think, because I am the most beautiful fish in the deep blue sea!*

● Read on to the end of the story. Organise the children into small groups. Encourage each group to hold a hot-seating session in order to reflect on the Rainbow Fish's behaviour and feelings at the end of the story.

> **Differentiation**
> **For older/more confident children:** Ask the children to write a character profile of the Rainbow Fish.
> **For younger/less confident children:** If necessary, ask a Learning Support Assistant to take on the role of the Rainbow Fish in order to model the process of hot-seating.

Plot, character and setting

Dive in

> **Objective:** To take turns to speak, listening to others' suggestions.
> **What you need:** *The Rainbow Fish*, CD player, 'watery' music, blue crêpe paper streamers hanging from the ceiling, a shell.
> **Cross-curricular links:** Drama

What to do
● Re-read the first page of the story. Ask the children to identify the words in the text that describe where the story is set. ('A long way out in the deep blue sea….')
● Explain that in this lesson you are going to take the children on a fantasy journey into the deep blue sea. Tell everyone to mime putting on their diving apparatus, diving into the water and swimming into the 'deep blue sea'.
● Encourage the children to use their senses to explore the imaginary underwater setting. Say: *Listen carefully. What can you hear?* (For example, a hermit crab scuttling across the rocks.) *Look all around. What can you see?* (Brightly coloured fish darting to and fro.)
● Tell everyone to swim back to shore and take off their diving suits. Sit in a circle. Pass a shell around the circle. Ask each child to describe something that they saw or heard in the deep blue sea, when it is their turn to speak. Encourage the children to be really inventive and imaginative in their vocabulary choices.

> **Differentiation**
> **For older/more confident children:** Write a detailed description of an underwater story setting.
> **For younger/less confident children:** Ask the children to write a list of all the things that they saw in the deep blue sea.

Illustrate the setting

> **Objective:** To make adventurous word and language choices appropriate to the style of the text.
> **What you need:** *The Rainbow Fish*, paper, pencils, crayons, felt-tipped pens.
> **Cross-curricular links:** Geography

What to do
● Ask the children to identify where the story of *The Rainbow Fish* is set. Encourage them to look for words and phrases in the text that describe the setting. ('Deep, blue sea', 'coral reef' and so on.) Write these words and phrases in a list on the board.
● Next, ask the children to draw a picture of an imaginary under-the-sea setting. Talk to the children individually as they are working on their pictures. Encourage them to describe the scene they are illustrating.
● Choose several of the children's pictures to display on the board. Invite the class to suggest some suitable descriptive words and phrases that could be used to describe the different scenes on display. Encourage the use of effective vocabulary that captures the atmosphere of the setting. Add the children's suggestions to the list on the board.
● Use shared writing to model a description of one of the children's pictures as a way of setting the scene for an underwater story.
● Finally, invite the children to write a short piece of text to describe the underwater setting they have drawn. Encourage them to incorporate some of the ideas on the board into their description if appropriate.

> **Differentiation**
> **For older/more confident children:** Show the children how to use a thesaurus to help them make interesting and appropriate vocabulary choices.
> **For younger/less confident children:** Encourage the children to annotate their pictures with words and phrases to describe each aspect of the scene they have drawn.

Plot, character and setting

Prized possessions

> **Objective:** To give some reasons why things happen or characters change.
> **You will need:** *The Rainbow Fish*, a copy of photocopiable page 18 for each child.
> **Cross-curricular links:** Citizenship

What to do

● As you re-read the story with the class, encourage the children to recall what happens next at relevant points.

● Point out the phrase 'prized possessions' on the final page. Discuss the Rainbow Fish's 'prized possessions'. What are they? Why are they so special to him? Why are the other fish envious of his special scales? Why didn't the Rainbow Fish want to give his scales away?

● Go around the circle and invite each child to give a brief description of their most treasured possession to the rest of the group. Ask the children to consider how they would feel if somebody asked them to give their special possessions away.

● Hand out photocopiable page 18 for each child to complete.

● Once completed, gather the group together to share ideas. Relate the discussion back to key events in the story. Consider whether it was fair of the other fish to expect the Rainbow Fish to share his shiny scales with them. Why/why not?

> **Differentiation**
> **For older/more confident children:** Organise the children into two groups to debate this question: *Do you think it was fair of the other fish to expect the Rainbow Fish to share his special scales with them?*
> **For younger/less confident children:** In shared writing, fill in photocopiable page 18 for a different story character. (For example, the giant's golden harp in *Jack and the Beanstalk*.)

Story bag

> **Objective:** To explore familiar themes through improvisation and role play.
> **You will need:** Digital camera; a cloth bag containing various items related to the story, such as shells, a toy starfish, pictures or photographs of an underwater scene (including cave), an octopus puppet, a Rainbow Fish with removable shiny scales, suitable 'watery' music.
> **Cross-curricular links:** Drama

What to do

● Introduce the story bag. Invite different children to take a story prompt out of the bag. Relate each item to a particular character, event or aspect of the story setting.

● Identify the order in which each of the pictures/objects appears in the story. Recognise that some of the story prompts will be used on more than one occasion.

● Help the children to re-enact the story using the various story prompts. Invite different children to retell a section of the story to the class. Ensure that the main events are presented in the correct sequence. Refer back to the shared text if necessary.

● Encourage the children to use story language, description and dialogue and to incorporate into their retelling suitable words and phrases that indicate the order of events in the story (for example, *one day, then, suddenly*).

● Use a digital camera to take some photographs of the children re-enacting the story. Use the photographs in a subsequent lesson to provide further opportunity to practise sequencing the main events in the story.

> **Differentiation**
> **For older/more confident children:** Consider how the oral re-telling differs from the original text.
> **For younger/less confident children:** Repeat the activity on several occasions in a small adult-led group. After each retelling, read the original version of the story to check that the order of events was correctly sequenced.

The Rainbow Fish

proud	**delighted**
kind	**selfish**
unhappy	**lonely**
upset	**happy**

SECTION
4

Problem-resolution stories

Plan your own story about someone who has a problem and asks for help.

● Title: _____

● Setting: _____

_____

_____

● Characters: _____

_____

_____

● What problem does the main character have? _____

_____

_____

● Who do they ask for help? _____

_____

_____

● What happens next? _____

_____

_____

_____

_____

SCHOLASTIC
www.scholastic.co.uk

Order, order!

The Rainbow Fish gave away his scales until he had just one special scale left.	No one would talk to the Rainbow Fish.
A little blue fish asked the Rainbow Fish for one of his special shiny scales.	The Rainbow Fish talked to the starfish.
The Rainbow Fish swam off to play with his new friends.	The Rainbow Fish gave the little blue fish a glittering scale.
The Rainbow Fish went to ask the octopus for advice.	The Rainbow Fish swam around the deep blue sea showing off his shimmering scales.

Plot, character and setting

Prized possessions

● Draw a picture of your 'most prized possession'.

● Describe your 'most prized possession'. _____

_____

_____

_____

● Write about how you would feel if someone tried to take your 'most prized possession' away. _____

_____

_____

_____

Talk about it

Feeling lonely

> **Objective:** To tell stories and describe incidents from their own experience.
> **What you need:** *The Rainbow Fish*, a copy of photocopiable page 22 for each child.
> **Cross-curricular links:** PSHE

What to do

● Show the children the page in the book that begins: 'What good were the dazzling, shimmering scales with no one to admire them?' Look at the illustration and read the text with the group. Ask the children to describe how the Rainbow Fish is feeling. (For example, *sad, upset, lonely* and so on.)

● Talk about why the Rainbow Fish is the 'loneliest fish in the entire ocean'. Why do none of the other fish want to play with him?

● Read on to the end of the story. Talk about how the Rainbow Fish's feelings change as the story progresses. Why is the Rainbow Fish no longer lonely?

● Invite each child to give an account of an occasion when they felt lonely and upset. Support younger or less confident children by asking some simple prompt questions, such as: *Why were you lonely? How did you feel? What did you do?*

● Provide each child with a copy of photocopiable page 22. Ask them to write about the experience they have just described to the group.

> **Differentiation**
> **For older/more confident children:** Read and discuss other stories which deal with the issue of loneliness (for example, *The Selfish Giant*).
> **For younger/less confident children:** Help the children to dramatise one of their experiences as a short role play.

People who help us

> **Objective:** To explain their views to others in a small group, and decide how to report the group's views to the class.
> **What you need:** *The Rainbow Fish,* paper and pencils.
> **Cross-curricular links:** PSHE/Citizenship

What to do

● Discuss with the children the key themes of the story described in *The Rainbow Fish*. Ask questions such as: *What problem did the Rainbow Fish have? How did he succeed in resolving this problem? Who helped the Rainbow Fish? What did they do?*

● Ask the children to share memories of a time when they needed help to overcome a particular problem. Encourage them to include details about what the problem was, who they turned to for help, and what happened next.

● Compile a list of 'people who help us' on the board. (For example: teacher, parent, friend, policeman, doctor, nurse.) Emphasise the fact that each type of person can help in different ways.

● Next, organise the children into small groups of three or four. Allocate to each group one of the 'people who help us' from the list on the board. Ask the children to discuss what kind of problems this person might help them to resolve.

● Nominate a scribe in each group to record the children's ideas.

● Finally, provide each group with an opportunity to report back the main points of their discussion to the rest of the class.

> **Differentiation**
> **For older/more confident children:** Ask the children to write a recount of an experience when they asked for help.
> **For younger/less confident children:** Help the children to prepare simple role plays based on their own experiences.

Talk about it

Help me!

> **Objective:** To act out a well-known story, using voices for characters.
> **You will need:** *The Rainbow Fish*. Drape a piece of dark material over a large table to create a gloomy cave.
> **Cross-curricular links:** PSHE/Citizenship, Drama

What to do

● Turn to the page in the story which begins 'I have been waiting for you…'. Look at the illustration and read the text together. Encourage the children to read the direct speech in a deep voice, as directed by the author.
● Working in pairs, instruct the children to act out this part of the story, focusing on the dialogue that takes place between the octopus and the Rainbow Fish.
● Circulate around the class. Listen to different pairs of children, offering encouragement and support as necessary. Ensure that the children speak in a manner appropriate to the role they are playing and keep the content of their dialogue pertinent to the story. Ask: *Do you think the Rainbow Fish would be speaking in a sad or happy voice? Why? What about the octopus?*
● Gather the class together. Choose different pairs of children to go into the cave and perform their dialogue to the rest of the class. Evaluate each performance.

> **Differentiation**
> **For older/more confident children:** Ask the children to write out the dialogue using speech marks to demarcate all direct speech.
> **For younger/less confident children:** Ask the children to record in a speech bubble one thing that their character said..

The Friendship Fish

> **Objective:** To take turns to speak and listen to others' suggestions.
> **You will need:** *The Rainbow Fish*, a copy of photocopiable page 23 for each child and one enlarged copy.
> **Cross-curricular links:** PSHE/Citizenship

What to do

● As you read through the story of *The Rainbow Fish* with the children, empathise with how the Rainbow Fish is feeling at different points in the story. Talk about why the author wrote the story of the Rainbow Fish. Establish that the story teaches children about the importance of friendship and sharing.
● Talk about why the Rainbow Fish had no friends. To prompt the discussion, ask the children questions such as: *Would you like to be friends with someone who didn't share their toys? Why not? What kind of person would you choose to be your friend?*
● Show the children photocopiable page 23. Tell them that, like the Rainbow Fish, the Friendship Fish has some very special scales. Each of the Friendship Fish's special scales contains a word that describes a quality of a good friend.
● Ask the children to suggest words and phrases that describe the attributes of a good friend. (For example, *loyal, fun, kind*.) List their ideas on the board. Pick five children to choose an adjective from the list and write it in one of the Friendship Fish's special scales (on an enlarged copy of photocopiable page 23).
● Working cooperatively in pairs, let the children design their own Friendship Fish using their own versions of photocopiable page 23.

> **Differentiation**
> **For older/more confident children:** Let the children use a dictionary to help with spellings.
> **For younger/less confident children:** Make a group Friendship Fish. Ask each child to record one characteristic of a good friend on a cardboard scale.

Talk about it

Underwater news

> **Objective:** To ask and answer questions, make relevant contributions and take turns.
> **You will need:** A recording of a television news report (if you have an ERA licence), a toy microphone and a video camera (optional).
> **Cross-curricular links:** ICT, Drama

What to do

● Watch a carefully selected news report. Consider the role of the presenter (introduces the story and recounts the main events) and the reporter (interviews people at the scene to find out more about what has happened).

● Tell the children that you would like them to help you turn the story of the Rainbow Fish into a news report.

● Sit in a circle. Begin retelling the story in the style of a news report. 'Earlier today in the deep blue sea…'. Pass the microphone around the circle, letting each child contribute a couple of sentences to develop the story.

● In pairs, ask the children to adopt the roles of a news reporter and a character from the story. Drawing on their knowledge of the story, the reporter should pose a range of simple questions for their partner to answer.

● Take on the role of presenter. Introduce each pair in turn. ('Now we can go over to our reporter ___ who is with ___ in the deep blue sea.') Let each pair perform their interview to the rest of the group.

● If possible, use a video camera to record the children's interviews to watch and evaluate in a subsequent lesson.

> **Differentiation**
> **For older/more confident children:** Ask groups of children to prepare and present a news report to the rest of the class.
> **For younger/less confident children:** Provide adult support during the paired activity.

Speech bubbles

> **Objective:** To explore familiar characters through role play.
> **What you need:** *The Rainbow Fish*, a copy of photocopiable page 24 for each pair of children, pencils.
> **Cross-curricular links:** Drama

What to do

● Ask the children to imagine that they are the Rainbow Fish. Begin reading the story. Pause at significant points in the narrative and let the children verbalise what they think the Rainbow Fish might be thinking or saying. (For example: *I don't want to play with you! GO AWAY! Please help me. Nobody wants to play with me.*) Encourage the children to speak clearly and with appropriate expression.

● Look at an example of a speech bubble in a picture book or comic. If necessary, remind the children that the words written inside a speech bubble show what a character is saying.

● Open the book at the illustration that shows the Rainbow Fish giving the little blue fish one of his shiny scales. Working in pairs, ask the children to discuss what the two fish might be saying to each other.

● Give each pair a copy of photocopiable page 24 and a pencil so that they can record their best ideas. Bring the group back together. Listen to each pair read out the text in their speech bubbles.

> **Differentiation**
> **For older/more confident children:** Model how to give emphasis to particular words and phrases by using bold print, capitals or exclamation marks when recording text in a speech bubble.
> **For younger/less confident children:** Let the children use a tape recorder to record their ideas.

Talk about it

SECTION

5

Feeling lonely

● The Rainbow Fish felt lonely because none of the other fish would talk to him. Write about a time when you felt lonely.

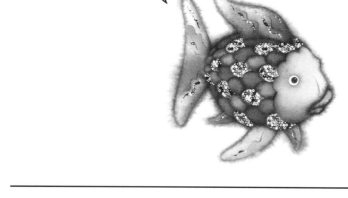

Why were you lonely?

How did you feel?

What happened?

_____

_____

_____

_____

_____

_____

_____

SCHOLASTIC
www.scholastic.co.uk

The Friendship Fish

- Work with a partner.
- Talk about the qualities that you think make a person a good friend.
- Write some of your ideas on the Friendship Fish's special scales.

Illustration © Baz Rowell / Beehive Illustration

Speech bubbles

● Look carefully at the picture. Imagine what the little blue fish and the Rainbow Fish are saying to each other.

● Write a sentence in each speech bubble to show what the fish are saying to each other.

Illustration © 1992, Marcus Pfister

Get writing

Come to my party

Objective: To select from different presentational features to suit particular writing purposes.
What you need: A copy of photocopiable page 28 for each child and one enlarged copy, pencils.

What to do
● Tell the children that the Rainbow Fish is having a party and he would like to invite all of his new friends.
● Let the children discuss and share their own experiences of sending and receiving party invitations. Consider what information it is important to include in an invitation. (Who the invitation is to and from, where and when the party will take place, and so on.)
● Display the enlarged copy of photocopiable page 28 on the board. Discuss the key information that needs to be filled in on each line.
● Fill in the invitation and direct it to a character

from the story (such as the little blue fish) as a shared writing activity. Ask the children to suggest when and where the party will take place. (The Shipwreck Café, an underwater bouncy castle.) In the space provided under the invitation, write a sentence giving additional information about what will happen at the party. (For example: We will play hunt the shell and eat seaweed sandwiches for tea.)
● Give out copies of photocopiable page 28. Ask the children to write a party invitation from the Rainbow Fish to one of the other characters in the story.

Differentiation
For older/more confident children: Get the children to swap invitations with a partner. Ask them to read the invitation and then write a reply.
For younger/less confident children: Ask a Learning Support Assistant to act as a scribe for the children.

Octopus fact-file

Objective: To maintain consistency in non-narrative, including purpose and tense.
You will need: A variety of sources of information about octopuses (non-fiction books, CD-ROMs, the internet or a simple self-prepared fact sheet), paper and pencils.
Cross-curricular links: Science

What to do
● Talk about what the children already know about octopuses. List the facts in note form on the board.
● Discuss with the children what else they would like to find out about these creatures. (For example, facts about appearance, feeding, behaviour and so on.)
● Provide opportunities for the children to research information about octopuses from a range of sources (see 'You will need' above). Organise the class to work in groups, pairs or

individually. Provide paper and pencils for the children to record simple notes.
● In a subsequent lesson, show the children how to use their notes to help them write and illustrate a simple fact sheet about octopuses.
● Model how to write a few of the children's ideas as simple factual sentences. For example: *If an octopus loses an arm it can grow another one to replace it. An octopus can change colour to hide from its enemies.*
● Remind the children to demarcate each sentence with a capital letter and full stop.

Differentiation
For older/more confident children: Show the children how to organise their writing under simple headings ('Appearance', 'Feeding' and so on).
For younger/less confident children: Ask each child to write and illustrate one interesting fact about octopuses. Bind the children's work together to make a group book.

Get writing

Kennings

> **Objective:** To create short simple texts that combine words with images.
> **You will need:** Enlarged copy of photocopiable page 29, paper and pencils.

What to do
● Share the poem 'Who am I?' on photocopiable page 29. Ask the children to identify which of the characters in *The Rainbow Fish* the poem describes.
● Now read each line of the poem in turn. Clarify the meaning of any unfamiliar vocabulary. Encourage the children to consider each two-word description in terms of their knowledge of the story. Ask: *Why was the Rainbow Fish a 'Proud swimmer'? Why does the author describe the Rainbow Fish as a 'Help seeker'? Who did he seek help from, and why?*
● Explain that this type of poem is called a 'kenning'. A kenning is a way of describing something without revealing what it actually is. In poetry, a kenning usually takes the form of a list made up of two-word descriptions of a person or object.
● Invite the children to help you write some additional lines for the poem. (For example: *Lonely swimmer, Colourful creature.*)
● Once you have done this, ask the children to write their own kenning poem about the Rainbow Fish (or another character in the story).

> **Differentiation**
> **For older/more confident children:** Ask the children to write kenning poems to link with topics being studied in other subjects.
> **For younger/less confident children:** Provide the children with a simple writing frame, such as:
> ___ swimmer
> ___ swimmer
> Ask them to write a different word to describe the Rainbow Fish on each line.

Directions

> **Objective:** To maintain consistency in non-narrative, including purpose and tense.
> **You will need:** Copies of photocopiable page 30 for each child and one enlarged copy, paper and pencils.
> **Cross-curricular links:** Geography

What to do
● Display an enlarged copy of photocopiable page 30 on the board. Look at the map together. Explain that the Rainbow Fish used this map to help him find his way from the starfish to the octopus's cave.
● Read the written directions together. Invite several children to help draw the specified route on the plan.
● Talk about how the directions have been written. Draw attention to some of the key structural features of instructional texts that are illustrated by the shared text. (Clear statement of purpose; use of short, concise sentences written in the imperative; sequential steps set out in a numbered list; use of time words to reinforce chronological order.)
● Hand out copies of photocopiable page 30. Instruct the children to plan and draw a different route that the Rainbow Fish could take to get to the octopus's cave on their own copy of the map on the photocopiable sheet.
● Give out paper and pencils. Ask the children to produce a set of written directions to describe the route they have drawn, based on the model discussed in the shared text work.

> **Differentiation**
> **For older/more confident children:** Ask the children to follow and evaluate a partner's directions.
> **For younger/less confident children:** Ask the children to describe a route orally to a partner.

Get writing

Underwater adventure

> **Objective:** To draw on knowledge and experience of texts in deciding and planning what and how to write.
> **You will need:** *The Rainbow Fish*, paper and pencils.

What to do
● Spend a few minutes looking at the illustrations in the book and discussing the setting. Ask the children to think about how the setting has influenced the characters and events in the story.
● Brainstorm ideas for a different story in this setting. Ask the children to suggest other creatures (real or imagined) that might be found in the 'deep blue sea' and what kind of stories might take place there. (For example: A deep sea diver finds a treasure chest in an old shipwreck. A dolphin caught in a fishing net is rescued by a young mermaid.)

● Use shared writing to plan an underwater story. The plan should include a list of characters, a description of the story setting and a brief plot summary.
● Ask each child to plan their own story, drawing on the ideas introduced in the class discussion. Let them share their plans, describing their chosen character and explaining what will happen.
● The children can now write their own underwater story, beginning with a brief description of the story setting.

> **Differentiation**
> **For older/more confident children:** Write a sustained story using knowledge of key story elements (settings, characterisation, dialogue, language of story).
> **For younger/less confident children:** Ask children to draw a series of pictures to represent the key events, writing a simple caption beneath each picture.

Thank-you letter

> **Objective:** To use capital letters and full stops when punctuating simple sentences.
> **You will need:** *The Rainbow Fish*, paper and pencils.
> **Cross-curricular links:** Citizenship, ICT

What to do
● After you have read the story with the children, ask: *Why was the Rainbow Fish upset? Who did he ask for help? How did the octopus help the Rainbow Fish? Did the story have a happy ending? Why?*
● Working in pairs, ask the children to discuss how the Rainbow Fish could express gratitude for the help he received from the octopus. (For example, a card, a letter, an email or by returning to the cave to thank the octopus in person.)
● Encourage the children to consider what sort of things the Rainbow Fish might say to the octopus.
● Model how to write a short thank-you letter to the octopus, using ideas suggested by the children. For example:

> Dear Octopus,
> Thank you for helping me yesterday. I have given each of the other fish one of my shiny scales and now I have lots of friends to play with.
> From
> The Rainbow Fish

● Hand out paper and pencils. Ask the children to imagine they are the Rainbow Fish and write a thank-you letter to the octopus. Alternatively, let the children word-process a letter on the computer.

> **Differentiation**
> **For older/more confident children:** Provide envelopes and ask the children to invent an address to which to send their letter.
> **For younger/less confident children:** Complete the activity as a shared writing activity or provide a simple writing frame for the children to fill in.

Come to my party

Dear _____

Please come to my party on _____
Time _____
At _____

From _____
RSVP_____

_____

• _____
• _____
• _____
• _____

Illustration © 1992, Marcus Pfister

SCHOLASTIC
www.scholastic.co.uk

READ & RESPOND: Activities based on The Rainbow Fish

Kennings

Who am I?

Proud swimmer

Silent glider

Sad loner

Help seeker

Scale sharer

Shiny sparkler

Happy player

Text © Louise Carruthers

Get writing

SECTION
6

Directions

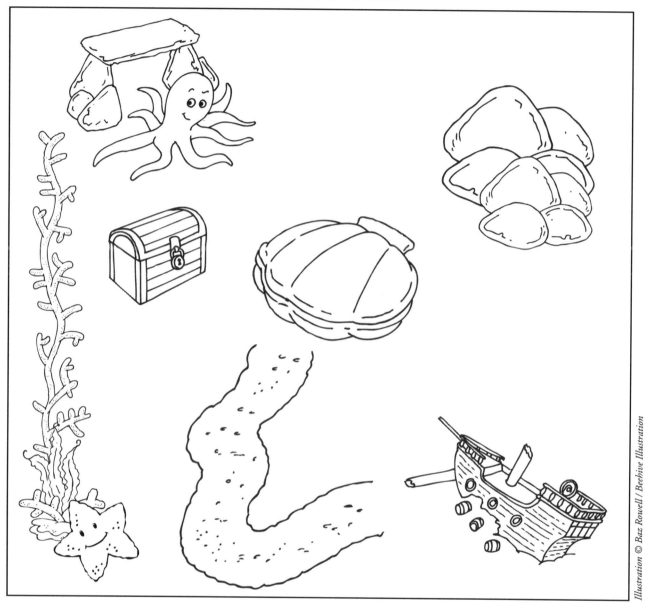

Illustration © Baz Rowell / Beehive Illustration

How to get to the Octopus's Cave

1. Start at the starfish.

2. Then swim towards the ancient shipwreck on your right.

3. Swim around the shipwreck and follow the sandy track towards the giant clam.

4. Next turn right and swim around the slippery rocks.

5. Finally, turn left to the octopus's cave.

Assessment

Assessment advice

Ongoing formative assessment of children's achievements and progress in literacy is essential. It enables teachers to make judgements about the progress that individuals are making towards achieving specific learning targets, and to plan future activities at an appropriate level.

Formative assessment for learning may take a variety of forms, including observations, discussion and questioning, analysis of children's work and peer-assessment or self-assessment. Children's performance in all of the activities in this book can be evaluated using one or more of the above assessment techniques.

Each of the teaching ideas in *Read and Respond: The Rainbow Fish* has a clear, assessable learning objective, which states what it is aimed that children should know/be able to do by the end of the lesson. In order to involve pupils fully in their learning, it is important that teachers share the learning objective with the children at the beginning of each activity.

At the end of an activity, it is important to help the children reflect back to the learning objective in order that they may understand what they have done well and where they will go next with their learning.

The activity on photocopiable page 32 requires the children to write an account of the events in the narrative from the Rainbow Fish's perspective. It provides a framework for assessing children's ability to:

1) write in sentences
2) recall significant incidents in the story
3) sequence the main events in order
4) use a range of time connectives appropriately.

Dear diary

Assessment focus: To write a chronological text using simple structures.
What you need: A copy of photocopiable page 32 for each child, an enlarged set of the plot cards on photocopiable page 17 (for younger/less confident children).

What to do
● Working together, arrange the plot cards in order on the board. Invite different children to retell a section of the story to the class, using the plot cards as prompts. Encourage the children to speak in sentences and to use appropriate time connectives to link events.
● Show the children a copy of photocopiable page 32. Talk about what a diary is used for. (It is a personal record of events that have taken place on a particular day.) Ask the children to guess who the diary belongs to. (The Rainbow Fish.)
● Provide each child with a copy of photocopiable page 32. Explain that you would like everyone to write a recount of the events in the story in the style of a diary entry written by the Rainbow Fish.

● Before the children begin writing, remind them to:

1) recount the main incidents in the story in chronological order;
2) use time words to connect events;
3) include description of setting, characters and feelings;
4) write in complete sentences demarcated with capital letters and full stops.

Differentiation
For younger/less confident children: Ask the children to order a set of the plot cards provided on photocopiable page 17 and then write a sentence under each picture. Alternatively, the children could be asked to give an oral recount of events from the Rainbow Fish's perspective.

Dear diary

This morning I was swimming in the deep blue sea when...

_____

_____

_____

_____

_____

_____

_____

_____

_____

_____

_____

_____

_____